the amazing human body

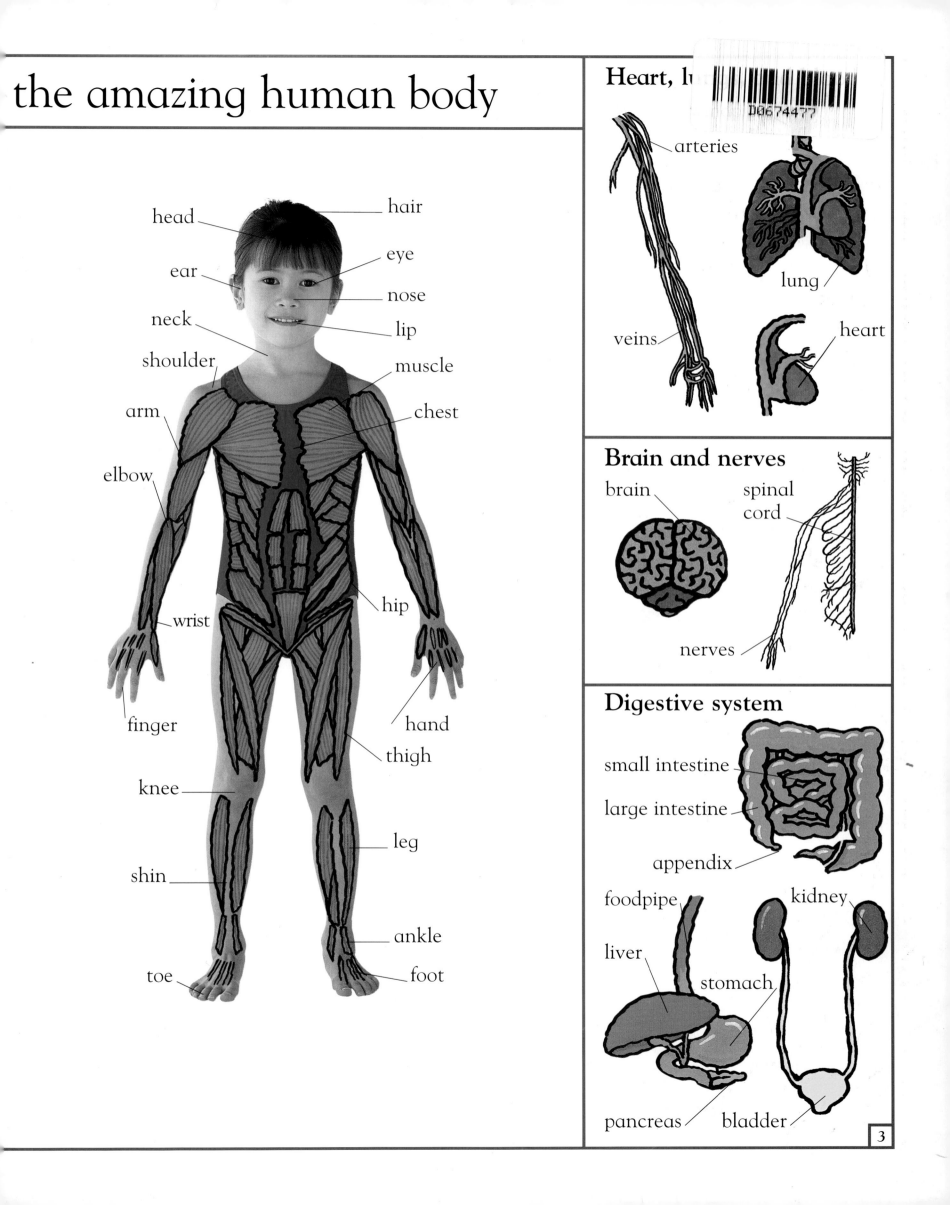

head
hair
ear
eye
nose
neck
lip
shoulder
muscle
arm
chest
elbow
wrist
hip
finger
hand
thigh
knee
leg
shin
ankle
toe
foot

Heart, lungs

arteries
veins
lung
heart

Brain and nerves

brain
spinal cord
nerves

Digestive system

small intestine
large intestine
appendix
foodpipe
kidney
liver
stomach
pancreas
bladder

3

DK

A DORLING KINDERSLEY BOOK

Note to Parents and Teachers

In **My First Body Book**, each body system is introduced by a paragraph that explains its basic functions. Interactive games and activities then give a practical demonstration of how the different body parts work. You can help children to make their own discoveries by encouraging them to relate the information in this book to their own bodies.

See-through section

The see-through pages have been designed so that children can look right inside a body and see where each part belongs. The labels will help children to identify and learn the names of different body parts.

Editor Lara Tankel Holtz
Senior Art Editor Penny Britchfield
Managing Editor Sheila Hanly
Production Marguerite Fenn, Fiona Baxter

Photography by Steve Shott, Paul Bricknell
Illustrations by Ellis Nadler
Medical Consultant Dr. Caroline Hoffbrand

First published in Great Britain in 1995
by Dorling Kindersley Limited,
9 Henrietta Street, London WC2E 8PS

A CIP catalogue record for this book
is available from the British Library

ISBN 0-7513-5330-2

Colour reproduction by Colourscan
Printed in Belgium by Proost

Acknowledgments
Dorling Kindersley would like to thank the following for their help in producing this book:
Robert Paul Mackenney FRCS, and Dr. Ganesh Supramaniam at Watford General Hospital; Helen Melville; Karen Fielding; Tim Lewis; Sue Unger at Frank Barnes School; Cathleen Gaster at Linden Lodge School; Broadfields Infants School; Sarah Leader; Katie Blumhof; Dr. Susan Cunningham.

Dorling Kindersley would like to give special thanks to the following for appearing in this book:
Andrew Berkhut; Vanessa, Cory, Alex, Stephen, and Ethan Chivers; Gregory Coleman; Acer Ganley; Vinae Gulrajani; Dilan Himtocha; Mark Islin; Sam Keis; Terry Kelly; Amber and Chloe Kenner; Helen Lane-Milner; Leanne Lau; Mathew and Mark Leader; Rosie Levine; Gala Marciandi; Joseph Mills; Richard Monan; Toni Palmer; Meera Patel; Sam Priddy; Maxwell Ralph; Lilli Risner; Elizabeth Robert; Pia Sarker; Kesavan Srikanthan; Barrie Tankel; Yasmin Vaughn; Ahmani Vidal-Simon; Jack Winer.

Additional photography by:
Susanna Price; Dave King; Tim Ridley; Steve Gorton; Geoff Brightling; Philip Dowell; Jo Foord; Frank Greenaway; Stephen Oliver; Jerry Young.

CONTENTS

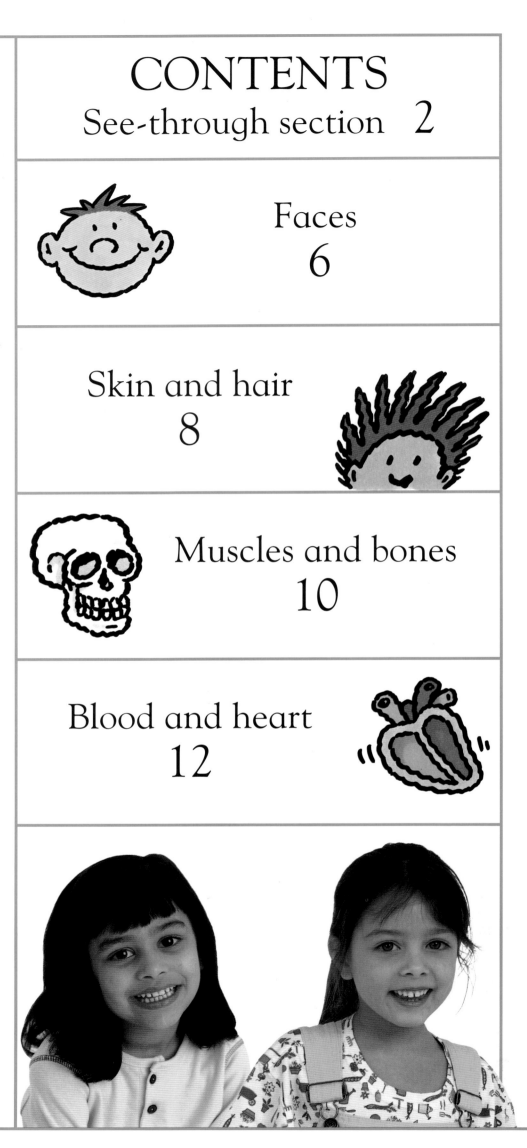

Chimpanzees and humans use their faces to show how they feel – a smile means they're happy, but a chimpanzee laughs when it's angry or sad.

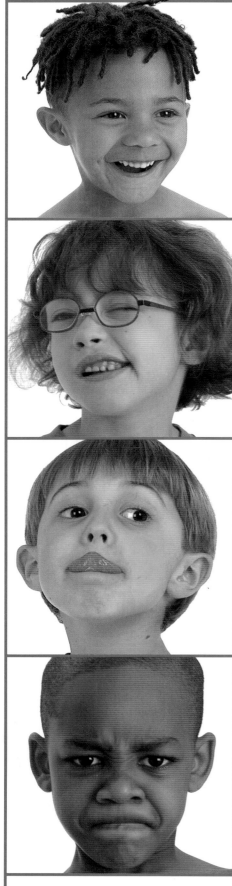

Faces

There are about five billion people in the world and every one has a different face. The colour of your eyes, hair, and skin, and the shape of your nose, are things that make you look special.

Two-faced
The line of your nose divides your face but the two halves are not exactly the same.

Hold a mirror in the middle of a photo of yourself. Look at the reflection on both sides. Do you seem to have two different faces?

Face fit
When police try to identify suspects in a crime they make pictures from different face parts such as the hair, eyes, nose, and mouth. Can you do the same?

- Ask a friend to think of someone you both know, such as a teacher at school.
- Take turns in drawing parts of the face, folding over the paper as you draw each part.
- When the face is complete open it up.

Can you recognize the person? See if other friends can guess who it is.

How do you feel?
We use our faces to show how we feel. Look in a mirror and see how many different faces you can make. Try sad, surprised, silly, happy, and angry faces.

The first false teeth were worn in Italy in about 700 BC. They were made of bone, ivory, or wood.

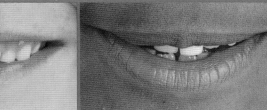

Teeth

You use your teeth to bite and chew food. At first you have 20 teeth, called milk teeth. At about the age of six your milk teeth will start to wobble and fall out. Thirty-two adult teeth will eventually grow in their place.

Bite size

Each tooth has a different job to do.

Incisors are like scissors. They have sharp edges for cutting up food.

Molars are like nutcrackers. They crush and grind food into small pieces.

Canines are like jagged knives. They are sharp and pointed for tearing.

incisors cut and slice

molars crush and grind

gum seals the top of the tooth inside the jaw

canines tear and spear

Inside a tooth

Each tooth is covered in a shiny, hard coating called enamel. Inside is a soft pulp made of blood vessels and nerves. Roots hold teeth firmly inside the jawbone.

enamel

pulp

gum

jaw-bone

root

Toothache

When you eat, tiny pieces of food get stuck in your teeth. After a while the sugar in these scraps of food make acids, which rot your teeth and may give you toothache. Brushing and flossing your teeth helps to keep your teeth and gums strong and healthy.

On your 70th birthday you will have enamel that was formed in your mother's womb – tooth enamel does not change throughout your life.

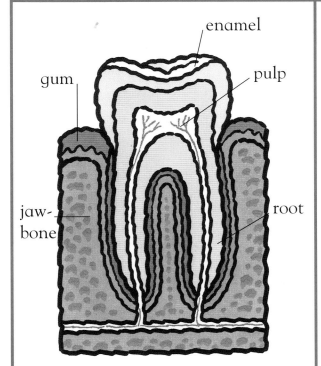

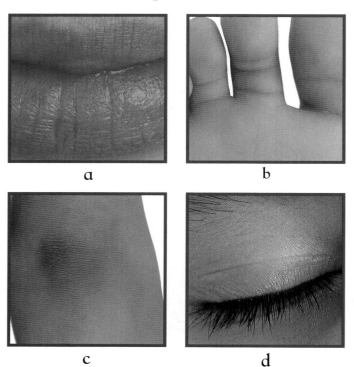

Skin and hair

Your skin protects your body from the outside world. It helps to keep out harmful germs and make sure you stay warm or cool. Little hairs grow all over your skin, except on your lips, palms, and soles of your feet.

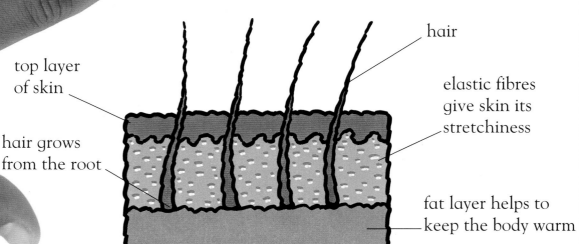

hair

top layer of skin

elastic fibres give skin its stretchiness

hair grows from the root

fat layer helps to keep the body warm

Skin parts

Skin doesn't look the same all over your body. The skin on your elbow is more wrinkly than the skin on your face. Do you know which parts of the body these sections of skin are from? The answers are printed below.

a

b

c

d

a. lips b. toes c. elbow d. eyelid

Watertight

Skin keeps water and body fluids inside your body. Oil in the skin helps to make it waterproof. Fingers and toes don't make oil – that's why they wrinkle up if you stay in water too long.

Every day, millions of dead skin cells flake off your body.

Your skin weighs about three kilograms – as much as a small bag of potatoes.

As you grow, your skin grows with you so that it always fits like a glove.

Sweat and shiver

Skin helps to keep your body at the right temperature. When you are hot, your skin sweats salt water to cool you down.

Hair helps to keep you warm. If you are cold, tiny hairs stand on end, trapping warm air and making goose bumps.

Skin care

The sun makes harmful rays which can damage your skin. Always protect yourself from the sun by wearing a hat and a sunscreen.

Be a fingerprint detective

Everyone has fingerprints, but no two are the same. Detectives look at fingerprints at the scene of a crime to help them to identify the criminals. See if you can spot your own fingerprint.

- Colour the end of a finger with a pen. Press firmly on to a sheet of paper. Ask your friends to make finger-prints on the same piece.
- When the sheet is covered in prints look at the lines on your fingers. See if you can match them with the prints you made.

| arch | loop | whorl |

Which of these patterns are most like your prints? The arch, the loop, or the whorl?

Head of hair

Hair comes in all shapes, lengths, and colours. Curly, long, brown – what does your hair look like?

If your hair is blond, you have about 140,000 hairs on your head. If you have red hair, you will only have about 90,000 hairs. If your hair is brown or black, you have about 110,000 hairs.

The hair on your head grows about two millimetres a week – that's about as long as the tip of a pencil.

The skin on your eyelid is 0.5 millimetres thick – as thin as a hair. On the sole of your foot your skin is six millimetres thick – as thick as a slice of bread.

Muscles and bones

If you could peel your skin back like a banana skin, you would find muscles and bones underneath it. These work together so that you can run, walk, breathe in and out, bend over, or jump up and down. Without muscles and bones you would not be able to move at all.

Bendy bones
When you stretch, bones support your body while muscles pull the bones into new positions.

Skeleton
There are 206 bones inside your body. They join together to make a skeleton. Every bone has a special job to do.

skull bone is like a crash helmet – it protects your brain

the top of your arm bone fits into a hollow in your shoulder bone – here it can turn around so you can throw a ball

27 bones in each hand help you to pick up and hold things

Muscle power
You have about 600 muscles in your body, all with different jobs to do – from your neck muscles that turn your head, to your toe muscles that help you walk.

arm muscles lift and pull

rib bones make a cage to protect your heart and lungs

spine is made up of lots of small bones called vertebrae – they keep you upright

thighbone is the longest in your body

Muscle memory

Ask a friend to press down on your arms while you press up as hard as you can. Count to 60. Ask your friend to let go. Your arm muscles will remember the downward push for a few seconds and your arms will float up by themselves.

Bag of bones

Your skeleton is a strong, jointed frame that holds you up and protects your insides. Without your bones you would be like a bag of wobbly jelly.

Broken bones

A doctor may wrap a broken bone in a plastic cast. The cast holds the broken ends of the bone together until they mend.

break

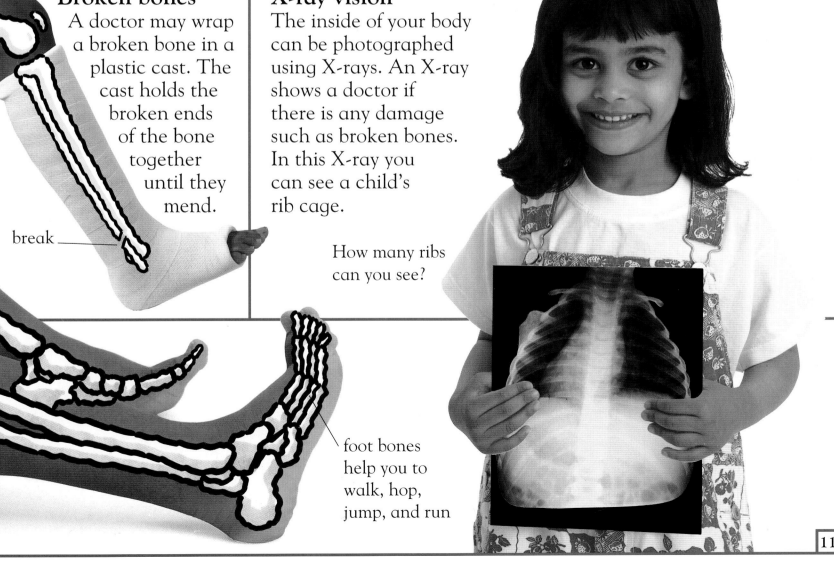

foot bones help you to walk, hop, jump, and run

Can you do this?

Your muscles help you to walk and run, but what else can they do?

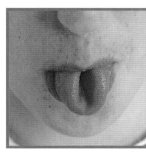

Can you roll up your tongue?

Can you raise one eyebrow or two?

The muscles in your thumbs help you to hold things. Can you do up the buttons on your shirt without using your thumbs?

X-ray vision

The inside of your body can be photographed using X-rays. An X-ray shows a doctor if there is any damage such as broken bones. In this X-ray you can see a child's rib cage.

How many ribs can you see?

You shrink by up to one centimetre during the day. Your vertebrae are squashed together by your weight. When you sleep your spine stretches out again.

The muscles in your eyes are very busy – they move more than 100,000 times a day.

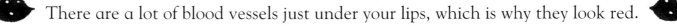

vein

heart

artery

Blood and heart

Your heart is a large muscle about the size of a fist. It pumps blood all around your body through blood vessels called arteries and veins. Arteries take healthy things such as air and food to different parts of your body, and veins carry away the unwanted things.

On the move
Blood travels in blood vessels to every part of your body.

Listen to your heart
A doctor uses a stethoscope to check that your heart and lungs are working properly. You can make your own stethoscope. Ask an adult to help you.

You will need

funnel

tape

scissors

three pieces of tubing, about 30 cm long

three-way hose connector

- Push one of the tubes into the funnel. Fit the other end into the hose connector.

- With an adult's help push one end of each of the other tubes into the hose connector.

- Listen carefully to the gentle beat of your friend's heart.
- Listen after your friend has jumped up and down ten times. Does the heart sound louder and faster?

- Hold the funnel firmly in the middle of your chest.

firmly tape the ends

12

Feel the beat

Press two fingers firmly on the inside of your wrist beneath your thumb. You can feel the throb, or pulse, of your heart pumping blood around your body. Can you see the blood vessels under your skin?

pulse can be felt here because blood vessels are close to the skin

Why do you blush?

When you are hot or feel shy, the blood vessels under your skin widen so more blood flows to your face, turning it red.

Cuts and scabs

If you cut your knee, a blood vessel breaks and you bleed. Blood stops germs from getting inside your body by making a sticky patch, called a clot. The dried clot, or scab, falls off when the cut has healed.

cut

scab

Bruises

If you knock yourself hard, a blood vessel breaks under the skin and blood leaks out. This turns your skin a bluey colour, called a bruise.

bruise

Germ control

Cuts and grazes should be washed to stop the dirt getting in. A plaster helps to keep germs out.

On the pulse

Your heart does not always beat at the same speed.

• Make a pulse chart like the one below.

• Take your pulse after doing quiet things and active things. Each time count the beats you feel in ten seconds.

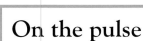

running	jumping	reading	sleeping
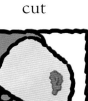			
19	16	13	11

• Use a watch with a second hand to time ten seconds.

Does the number of beats you feel stay the same or change?

Your heart beats about 80 times a minute, 4,800 times an hour, 115,200 times a day, and 806,400 times a week.

13

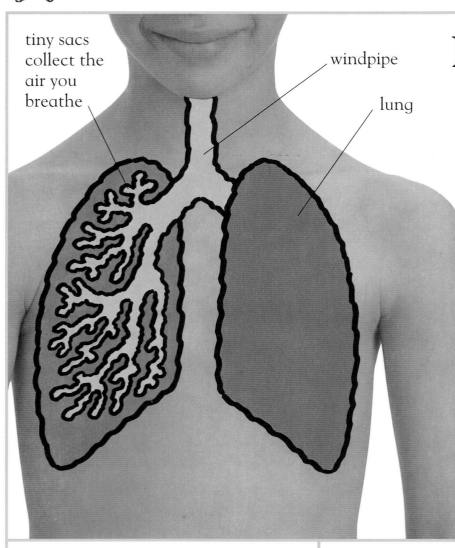

tiny sacs collect the air you breathe

windpipe

lung

Lungs and breathing

Your body needs air to stay alive. You breathe in air through your mouth and nose. As you breathe in, your ribs move out, so your lungs can fill with clean air. The air travels down your windpipe and into your two lungs.

When you breathe out, your ribs sink back and stale air is squeezed out through your nose and mouth. Put your hand on your chest and feel it moving in and out as you breathe.

Misty mirror

The air you breathe out is warm and wet. Breathe on to a mirror and watch it mist up. Now rinse your mouth with cold water and try again. What happens?

Full of air

How much air do you have in your lungs? Take a deep breath and blow into a balloon until you run out of air. How big is the balloon? This is about half the air in your lungs.

14

A large muscle underneath your lungs, called the diaphragm, jerks up and down when you laugh.

Noisy air

As you let air out of a balloon, the balloon vibrates, making a loud noise. When air from your lungs passes over vocal cords in your throat, the cords vibrate, making sounds. If you blow air through your lips, they vibrate and you whistle.

shouting

singing

whispering

whistling

Why do you yawn?

A yawn is the body's way of getting more air to make you feel more lively. When you yawn you breathe deeply and your lungs fill up with air.

Asthma

In an asthma attack the small air passages in the lungs get smaller and it is hard to breathe. Taking medicine or breathing it in from an inhaler can help.

Puff power

Use your lung power to race a car.

- Make two paper sails and tape them to straws.
- Tape the straws to two small, light toy cars.
- Race them across a table by blowing into the sails.

Sometimes you get hiccups if you eat or drink too quickly. Air suddenly rushes into your lungs and your vocal cords snap shut – hic!

15

When you sleep you breathe about 12 times a minute, but when awake you breathe about 18 times a minute.

Digestion

The food you eat is broken up into tiny pieces so your body can take out the goodness it needs. This process is called digestion. It starts as soon as you take a bite.

1 The apple is broken up by your teeth and mixed with saliva. It is now small enough to swallow.

2 The broken up apple slides down your foodpipe until it reaches your stomach.

3 In your stomach the apple mixes with juices until it turns into a thick, chunky liquid.

4 Over the next six hours, the apple soup flows through your intestines. From here, the things you need – water, vitamins, and sugar – are absorbed into your blood.

5 The leftovers are then pushed out of your body through your rectum when you go to the toilet.

Journey's end
Digestion starts at your mouth and ends at your rectum.

It takes about 24 hours to digest one meal.

In one year you will eat about 500 kilograms of food – that's about the weight of a small car.

 Pardon me! You burp when a bubble of air rushes up to your mouth from your stomach.

Eating well

To keep your body healthy and fit you need to eat a balanced diet. That means eating food from the following groups every day.

Building blocks

Fish, meat, cheese, and milk contain proteins. They help your body to repair itself and grow strong.

Energy

Bread, rice, and potatoes all give you energy. They are called carbohydrates. They help your body to move and work properly.

A little fat

Foods such as butter, oil, and avocados contain fat. A small amount of fat will give you energy, but too much fat is unhealthy.

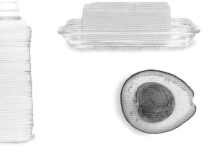

An apple a day

Vegetables and fruit contain vitamins and minerals. Eating lots of these every day helps you to stay healthy.

Thirsty work

Without water you cannot survive. Your body needs lots of water every day, so make sure you drink plenty of liquids.

Leftovers

Your kidneys turn water your body does not want into urine. Tubes take urine to your bladder. When your bladder is full you go to the toilet to empty it.

kidney

bladder

Staying alive

Food gives you the energy your body needs to run, jump, and even sleep. You need lots of energy to ride a bicycle, but less when you are drawing quietly.

If your intestines were stretched out in a straight line, they would be more than six metres long – you'd be a giant!

You hear a gurgling sound, like water running down a drain.

Your tummy rumbles when gas and juices churn through your digestive system.

Every day your body loses between one and two litres of water, through going to the toilet and sweating.

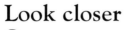
brain

Brain and nerves

Inside your head is your brain.
It looks like a cauliflower and is
about the size of your two fists.
Your brain controls your thoughts,
movements, and memory.

   Messages are sent to and
from your brain by nerves.
Nerves act like telephone
wires, letting your brain
know what is happening
to you. Your brain then
tells your nerves what
your body should do.

What a nerve
Nerves connect every part
of your body with your brain.

Look closer
Can you guess what these objects are by
looking at the photographs? Your brain
will help you to remember where you
have seen them before. The answers
are printed below.

a

b

c

d

a. pine cone b. toothbrush
c. balloon d. ball of string

The forgetting game
You can remember some things, such as your
name, for your whole life. Other things you
remember for just a few minutes. Look at these
ten objects for one minute. Now close the book
and see how many objects you can remember.

18

Seeing things

Your brain tries to make sense of what you're seeing, but it can make mistakes. An optical illusion is a picture that confuses your brain. These pictures are not quite what they seem.

Flower power

Look at the circles in the middle of these flowers. Do they look the same size? Now measure them with a ruler.

Seeing spots

Are there really spots between these black squares or is your brain confused?

Is it a bird?

Which can you see – a duck or a rabbit?

Teach your brain

Your brain finds some skills hard to learn. Try rubbing your tummy and patting your head at the same time. Does it get any easier if you practise?

Brain test

You will have to use your brain to work out what is wrong with these pictures. The answers are printed below.

a

b

c

d

e

a. missing finger on glove **b.** missing leg on spider **c.** numbers in wrong order **d.** two 12s on clock **e.** no spokes on bicycle wheel

Dreams are thoughts that you have while you are asleep. If you wake just as the dream ends, you will remember it – any later and you won't.

Some people have photographic memories. That means they could look at this page and remember every word on it.

19

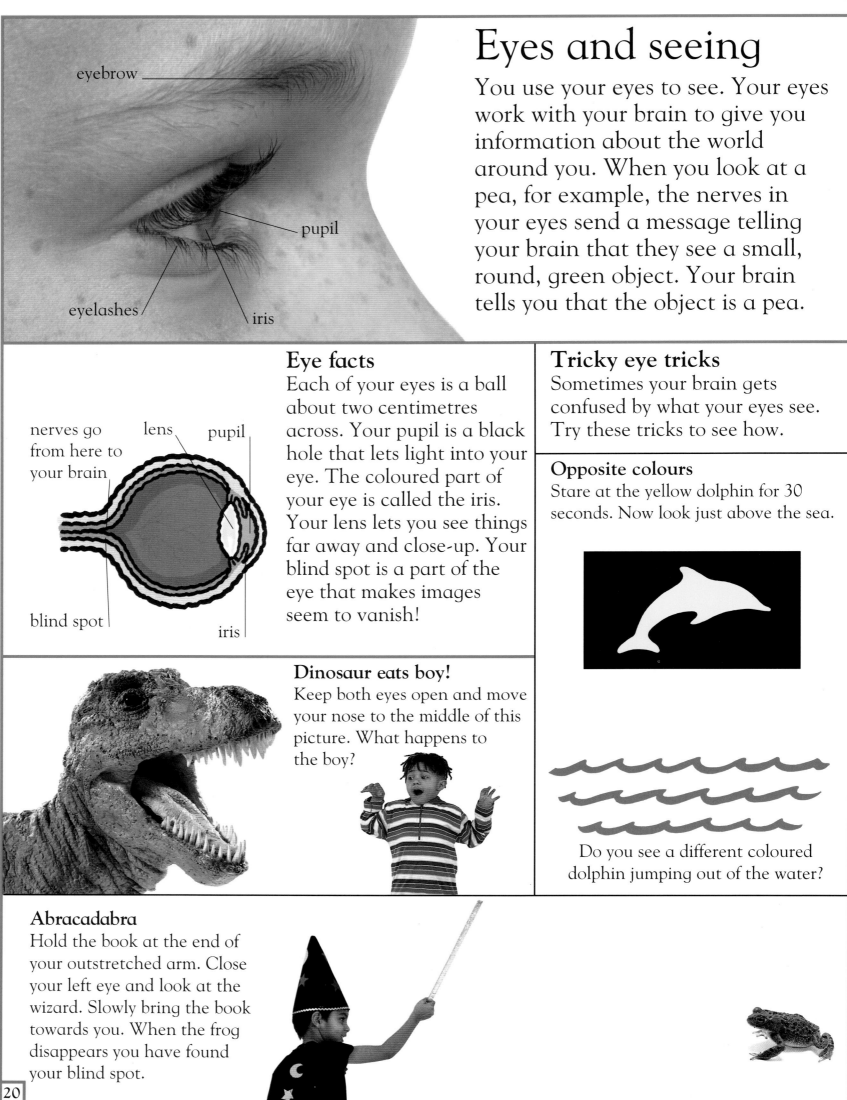

Eyes and seeing

You use your eyes to see. Your eyes work with your brain to give you information about the world around you. When you look at a pea, for example, the nerves in your eyes send a message telling your brain that they see a small, round, green object. Your brain tells you that the object is a pea.

eyebrow

pupil

eyelashes

iris

Eye facts

Each of your eyes is a ball about two centimetres across. Your pupil is a black hole that lets light into your eye. The coloured part of your eye is called the iris. Your lens lets you see things far away and close-up. Your blind spot is a part of the eye that makes images seem to vanish!

nerves go from here to your brain

lens

pupil

blind spot

iris

Tricky eye tricks

Sometimes your brain gets confused by what your eyes see. Try these tricks to see how.

Opposite colours

Stare at the yellow dolphin for 30 seconds. Now look just above the sea.

Dinosaur eats boy!

Keep both eyes open and move your nose to the middle of this picture. What happens to the boy?

Do you see a different coloured dolphin jumping out of the water?

Abracadabra

Hold the book at the end of your outstretched arm. Close your left eye and look at the wizard. Slowly bring the book towards you. When the frog disappears you have found your blind spot.

When something gets in your eye, tears are made to wash it away. Some tears fall on your cheeks and others drain away down your nose.

Carrots really do help you to see better. They contain special vitamins that can help you to see at night.

Reading by touch

People who cannot see read by feeling a bumpy alphabet of dots called Braille. Books with Braille and pictures can be shared by a blind and sighted child.

Spinning pictures

Sometimes your eyes see one picture when there are really two.

- Cut a circle of card and colour an insect on one side and a flower on the other.
- Make two holes on opposite sides of the circle and thread a loop of wool through each hole.
- Twist the circle and wool. Now pull the loops.

What happens to the insect and the flower?

Eye care

An optician tests your eyes to check whether you need to wear glasses. Protect your eyes with goggles when swimming, and never look directly at the sun.

Do you have a holey hand?

If one eye looks at one thing while the other eye looks at something else, your brain gets very confused.

- Roll up a piece of paper into a tube. Hold it in front of one eye.
- Put your other hand against the side of the tube near the end. Keep both eyes open and slide your hand towards you.

What happens to your hand?

Your pupils change size to let in more or less light. Look in a mirror, covering one eye. After 30 seconds uncover it and watch the pupil get smaller.

Eyelids act like windscreen wipers – when you blink, your eyelids spread a thin film of water over each eye.

nerves are deep inside here

stirrup bone

anvil bone

hammer bone

outer ear

eardrum

ear canal leads to eardrum

Ears and hearing

The main part of your ear is inside your head. The flappy outer ear you can see acts like a funnel, collecting sounds in the air and sending them into your ear canal. When sound reaches the eardrum, it vibrates. Nerves then send messages to your brain so that it can work out what you are hearing.

Tiny tools
The hammer is one of the smallest bones in your body.

Crossed wires
Soft noises can be difficult to hear clearly. Stand with friends in a line and whisper a message to the person next to you. Ask them to pass it on. What does the last person hear?

Do you need two ears?
Two ears help you find out where sound is coming from. Put on a blindfold and cover one ear. Ask a friend to tap a drum.

Can you point to the sound easily?

Who's calling?
Sounds are vibrations that can travel through things. Make a string telephone and hear the vibrations from a voice after they have travelled along the string from one pot to the other.

- Take a piece of string and two empty yoghurt pots.
- Make a small hole in the bottom of each pot.
- Push the string through each hole, then knot the ends.
- Keep the string tight and speak into one pot, while your friend listens in the other.

The sound from your voice

We can't hear our own voices the way other people do because some of what we hear vibrates inside our head.

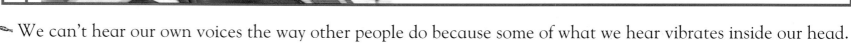

Helping to hear

If you have difficulty hearing, you may need a hearing aid. This is a tiny machine that fits into your ear to make sounds louder and clearer.

Sign language

People who are deaf can use sign language to communicate. Every country has a different sign language. This child is using British signs.

Hello!	My
name is	Lilli.

Feeling dizzy

When you spin round, the liquid deep inside your ears spins too. But when you stop, the liquid in your ears keeps spinning for a while. This makes you feel dizzy. Try this test to see what happens inside your ears. Stir a glass of water very quickly with a straw and then let go. Both the straw and the water will carry on spinning.

use a straw to stir the water

... travels along the string.

23

Your ears can hear a wide range of sounds, from loud sounds such as a dish breaking, to low sounds such as a growl, or high sounds such as birds singing.

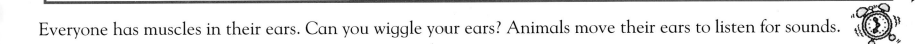

nerves in nose pick up smells

tongue tastes food

Taste and smell

Your sense of taste and smell work together. Your tongue is covered with thousands of tiny taste buds that pick out the tastes in food and drink. Your nose is packed with tiny hairs and nerves. The hairs trap smells and the nerves send messages about the smells to your brain. So when you bite an apple, your nose smells the flavour and your tongue tastes the sweetness.

Tongue tasters

The basic tastes of food are bitter, sweet, salty, and sour. You taste bitter things at the back of your tongue, sour in the middle, and salty and sweet at the tip.

bitter – like coffee   salty – like salt

sweet – like sugar   sour – like a lemon

Tongue test

Where on your tongue would you taste these things?

lime

orange peel

honey

crisps

Disguised smell

Taste is affected by what you smell.

- Ask an adult to chop an apple and potato.
- Put a blindfold on a friend. Hold an onion under her nose and then feed her some apple, then potato.

Can she taste the difference between the apple and the potato or does the onion confuse her?

Tasteless

When you have a cold, your food seems to lose some of its flavour. If your nose is blocked it's hard to smell – so you can't taste food properly.

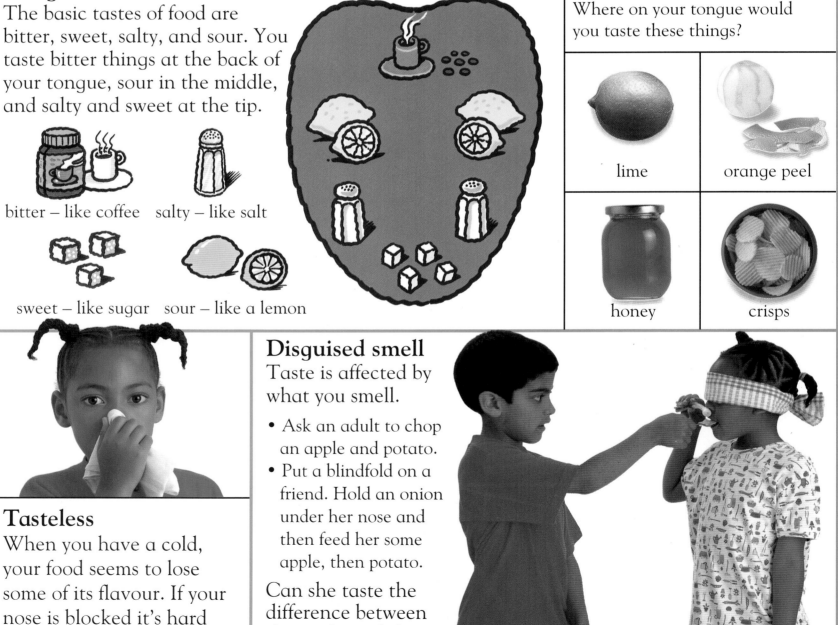

24

You have about 10,000 taste buds on your tongue, but by the time you are 60 nearly half of these will have died.

Funky fruit

You enjoy food because of how it looks, as well as how it tastes and smells. Would you like the taste of a purple banana or a silver lemon?

silver lemon

mauve orange

purple banana

blue pineapple

Dangerous smells

Your sense of smell warns you of danger. It tells you if there is a fire or if you are eating rotten food that will make you ill.

Can you think of other times when your sense of smell is useful?

Taste good?

It is harder to recognize the taste of food if you cannot see it.

• Put a variety of food on a plate.

• Blindfold a friend. Place the food on a spoon and carefully feed it to him.

• Ask your friend to guess what he's eating.

choose foods that have different tastes and smells

How many tastes did your friend recognize?

Your nose helps to exercise your body when you're asleep! If you sleep on your left side, your left nostril slowly gets blocked and your brain tells you to turn.

25

A dog's sense of smell is 32 times better than ours, but a shark can smell 11,000 times better than we can.

Your fingertips, lips, and tongue have more nerve endings than anywhere else in your body – this means that they are very sensitive to touch.

Touch

Your sense of touch tells you if there's a fly on your face or a stone in your shoe. Just under your skin are tiny nerves that feel things. In some places there are many nerves close together, making your skin very sensitive. Your fingertips have lots of nerves, but your back has only a few.

Escape the maze

Your fingertips are very sensitive. Can they find their way through this maze more quickly than your eyes?

- Trace the maze and make a path through it by pricking holes in the paper with a pin. Turn it over.
- Now let your fingertips find the way out.

Little box of horrors

You can recognize different things just by touching them. Can you imagine what the different parts of your body feel like?

- Make a hole in a big box.
- Collect some things that might feel like parts of a body.
- Try and convince your friends that they are feeling different parts of a body. They will be horrified!

Does the cauliflower feel like a crinkly brain?

write down the most horrible guesses

jelly feels like a heart

grapes feel like eyeballs

a carrot end is like a toe

spaghetti may feel like squiggly intestines

26

Guess who?
Can you recognize a friend's face just by touching it? Put on a blindfold. Use your hands to gently feel your friends' features. Can you guess whose face is whose?

Feely picture
Your skin can tell the difference between lots of different textures – rough, smooth, sharp, and soft. Make a feely picture with lots of things that feel different when you touch them.

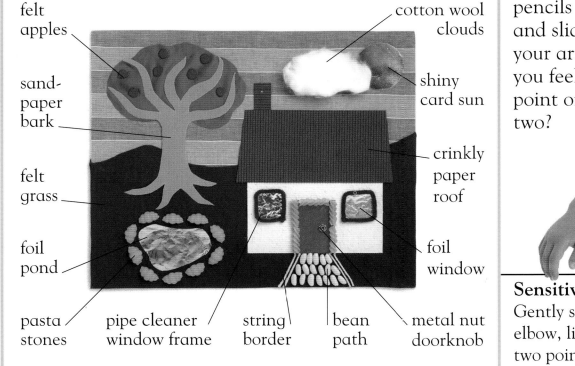

felt apples

cotton wool clouds

sand-paper bark

shiny card sun

felt grass

crinkly paper roof

foil pond

foil window

pasta stones

pipe cleaner window frame

string border

bean path

metal nut doorknob

Pencil test
In some places your skin is more sensitive than in others. Tape two pencils together and slide them up your arm. Can you feel one point or two?

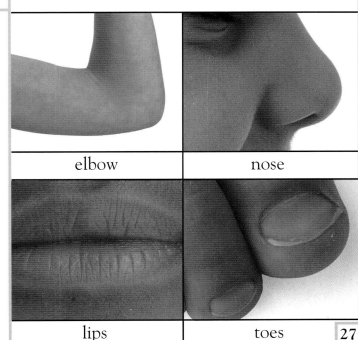

Sensitive skin
Gently slide the pencils on your nose, elbow, lips, and toes. Where can you feel two points and where can you feel one?

elbow	nose
lips	toes

Feel the difference
Touch tells you if things are hot or cold. But if you touch something hot and then touch something warm it will feel cold. Put one finger in a glass of hot tap water and one finger in a glass of cold water. Now put both fingers in warm water. Do they feel different?

cold warm hot

When skin is pressed for a long time you stop feeling the pressure. Tight socks will not hurt your legs, but look at the marks they leave on your skin!

If you knock your toe against something hard you will feel pain. Pain warns your brain that something is wrong.

Growing up

Even though you may not notice, you are growing all the time. You are getting taller, your limbs are becoming stronger, and your face is changing shape. As you grow, you learn about the world by watching and listening to other people. Some things, such as riding a bicycle, are learnt by practising.

Your changing body

When you are newborn you are almost helpless. As you grow older, you are able to do more things. Look at this person growing and changing. What makes him look older?

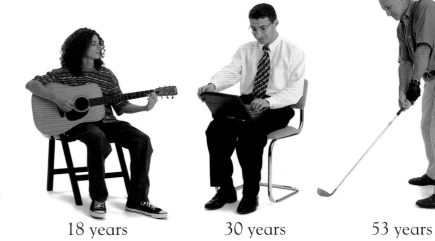

| 10 months | 7 years | 18 years | 30 years | 53 years |

How tall are you?

Everyone grows taller at different speeds. Make a height chart and measure your friends. Measure again in a month. Who's grown the most?

Watch them grow

Some parts of your body grow quickly and others slowly. Measure different parts of your body and discover the speedy growers.

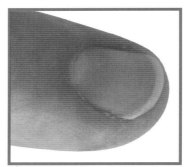

Measure a nail with a ruler every day.

Measure the length of your hair every week.

Put a tape measure around your head every two weeks.

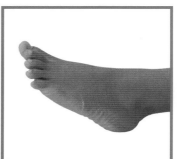

Draw around your feet and measure them every month.

28

You'll continue growing until you are in your teens. Girls tend to grow faster than boys, but boys grow for longer.

How you were born

A baby starts when a tiny sperm from the father joins with an egg inside the mother. The baby that starts to grow is called a foetus. It grows inside its mother's womb for nine months. After one week the baby is no bigger than the full-stop at the end of this sentence.

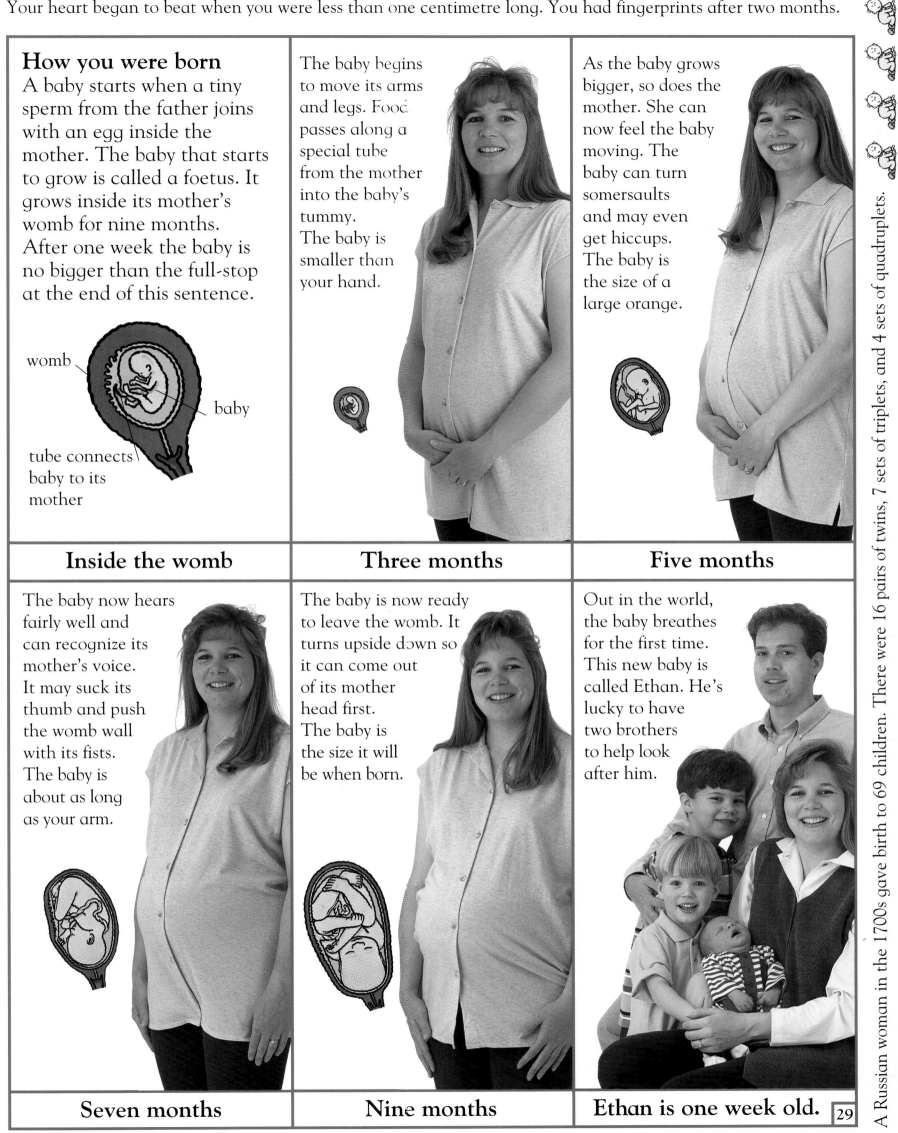

womb

baby

tube connects baby to its mother

Inside the womb

The baby begins to move its arms and legs. Food passes along a special tube from the mother into the baby's tummy.
The baby is smaller than your hand.

Three months

As the baby grows bigger, so does the mother. She can now feel the baby moving. The baby can turn somersaults and may even get hiccups.
The baby is the size of a large orange.

Five months

The baby now hears fairly well and can recognize its mother's voice. It may suck its thumb and push the womb wall with its fists. The baby is about as long as your arm.

Seven months

The baby is now ready to leave the womb. It turns upside down so it can come out of its mother head first.
The baby is the size it will be when born.

Nine months

Out in the world, the baby breathes for the first time. This new baby is called Ethan. He's lucky to have two brothers to help look after him.

Ethan is one week old.

29

A Russian woman in the 1700s gave birth to 69 children. There were 16 pairs of twins, 7 sets of triplets, and 4 sets of quadruplets.

All about you

No two people are the same.
Other people may look like you,
but no two faces are identical.
Other people may speak like
you, but no two voices are the
same. When you go to bed at
night you sleep and dream, but
even your dreams are different
from anyone else's.

Body map

Your body is made up of many parts. Each one
has its own job to do, but they all work together.
Make a body map to show where the different
parts belong in your body.

- Lie down on a large piece of paper.
- Ask a friend to draw around your body.

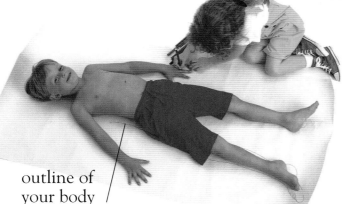

outline of
your body

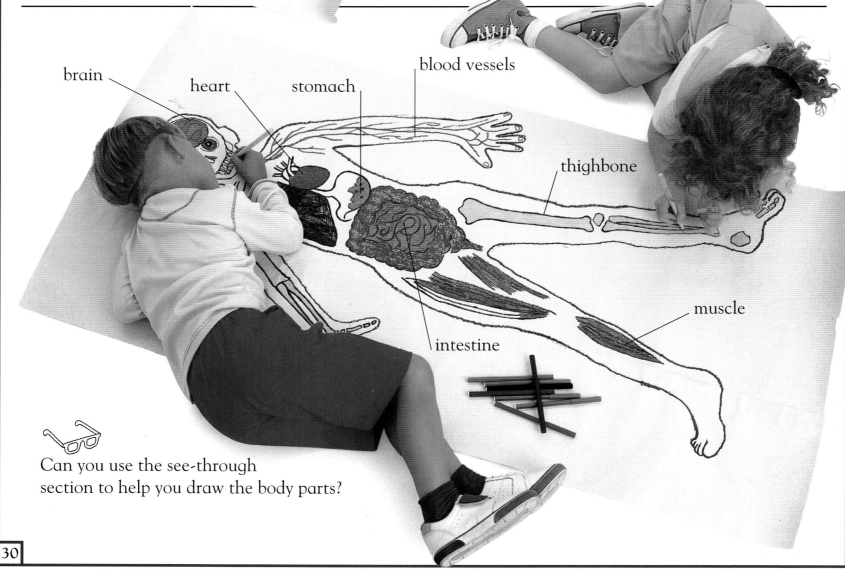

brain

heart

stomach

blood vessels

thighbone

muscle

intestine

Can you use the see-through
section to help you draw the body parts?

My scrapbook

Make a scrapbook all about yourself. Collect things about you and your family. Try and find out the first word you said. When did you learn to walk? Draw pictures of the things you like to do.

look at photographs of your parents when they were children

draw pictures of the people you live with

look at old photographs of your grandparents – do you look like them?

can you see a photo of this woman when she was younger?

What did you look like as a baby?

Have you got shoes from when you were a baby? Do they look very small?

Your only body

It is important to look after your body as you will have it for the rest of your life. Here are some ways to care for your body.

Eating well

You need to eat a balanced diet. This will give you the energy to play, grow, and stay healthy.

fruit and vegetables are healthy snacks

mask protects your lungs from dirt in the air

helmet protects your head

Sleeping

Sleep is important for a healthy body. It is the time when your body repairs itself and grows. It is also when your brain stores and sorts out the day's events. The younger you are the more sleep you will need.

Fit for life

Regular exercise makes your body strong and helps to protect you from illness. Running, playing sport, swimming, and riding a bicycle are all good ways to keep your body fit. What is your favourite way to exercise?

31

Where would you find the hardest substance in your body? Is your skin heavy? What does your skull do? Do you have more than 500 muscles?

Index